Children's Bible Stories

From the Old Testament

John Marshall

For information about permission to reproduce selections from this book, write to Permissions. The Light and the Way Books.

6845 Elm Street, McLean Va. 22101

Visit our Web site: WWW. Litchfield Literary Books.Com

THIS BOOK BELONGS TO_____

"Suffer the little children to come unto me, and forbid them not: for of such is the kingdom of God"

PREFACE

"The Children's Bible" provides, in simple English, a translation of selections from both the Old and the New Testament. These selections have been made as a result of more than twenty-five years of observation and study. The text is that of the Bible itself, but in the language of the child, so that it may easily be read to the younger children and by those who are older. It is not in words of one syllable, for while the child is reading the Bible he should gradually learn the meaning of new words and idioms.

The Bible contains the foundations on which the religious life of the child must be built. The immortal stories and songs of the Old and New Testaments are his richest inheritance from the past. To give him this heritage in language and form that he can understand and enjoy is the duty and privilege of his parents and teachers.

It is hoped that "The Children's Bible" will meet the need and the demand, which parents and educators alike have long felt and often expressed, for a simple translation of selections from the Bible most suited to the needs and the interests of the child. It is also believed that after the child has learned to appreciate and love these stories and songs, he will be eager and able to read the Bible as a whole with genuine interest and understanding.

INDEX TO STORIES

THE STORY OF CREATION

In the beginning God made the heavens and the earth, and while the earth was still unformed, God said, "Let there be light," and there was light. And God saw that the light was good. Then God separated the light from the darkness. And God called the light Day and the darkness Night. And there was an evening and a morning, making the first day.

And God said, "Let there be a sky and let it divide the waters that are below from the waters that are above the sky." And it was done. And God called the sky the Heavens. And there was an evening and a morning, making the second day.

And God said, "Let the waters under the heavens be brought together, and let the dry land appear." And it was done. And God called the dry land Earth and the waters that were brought together Seas. And God saw that it was good.

And God said, "Let plants and trees grow from the earth." And it was done. And plants and trees grew from the earth, each plant bringing forth its own kind of seed and each tree its own kind of fruit, and God saw that it was good. And there was an evening and a morning, making the third day.

And God said, "Let there be lights in the heavens to separate the night from the day. Let them be signs to mark the seasons, the days, and the years. Let them be lights in the heavens to light the earth." And it was done. So God made the two great lights (the sun and the moon): the greater to rule the day and the lesser to rule the night. God made the stars also and placed them in the heavens to throw light upon the earth. And God saw that it was good. And there was an evening and a morning, making the fourth day.

And God said, "Let the waters bring forth many living creatures and let birds fly above the earth and in the sky." And God made large sea-monsters and all kinds of living creatures with which the waters abound, and all kinds of birds. And God saw that it was good. And he blessed them, saying, "Increase and fill the waters in the seas, and let the birds increase on the earth." And there was an evening and a morning, making the fifth day.

And God said, "Let the earth bring forth all kinds of living creatures, cattle and creeping things and wild beasts." And it was done. So God made all the different kinds of wild beasts, and the cattle, and everything that crawls upon the ground. And God saw that it was good.

And God said, "Let us make man like ourselves. Let him rule over the fish in the sea, the birds of the sky, the cattle, the wild beasts and all the living things that crawl upon the ground." And God made man like himself, like God he made him. He made them male and female.

And God blessed them, and said to them, "Have children, increase, live all over the earth, and conquer it; rule over the fish of the sea, the birds of the sky, and over every living thing that crawls upon the ground."

And God said, "See, to you I give every plant which grows on all the earth, and every tree which bears fruit with its own kind of seed. It shall be food for you. And to every wild beast and to every bird of the sky and to every thing that crawls on the earth and is alive, I give every green herb for food." And it was done.

And when God saw everything that he had made, he saw that it was verygood. And there was an evening and a morning, making the sixth day.

And the heavens and the earth were finished and all that there was in them. And on the seventh day when God had finished the work which he had done, he rested from all his work. And God blessed the seventh day and made it holy, for in it he rested from all the work which he had done.

GOD'S GOOD GIFTS TO MAN

At the time when Jehovah made earth and heaven, no trees or plants grew on the earth, for Jehovah had not yet sent the rain; and there was no man to till the soil; but a mist rose from the earth and watered the ground.

Then Jehovah made man out of dust taken from the ground and breathed into him the breath of life; and man became a living being. And Jehovah planted a garden in Eden, far in the East; and out of the ground he made grow all kinds of trees that are pleasant to look at and good for food, also the tree of life and the tree that gives the knowledge of good and evil.

Then Jehovah took the man and put him in the garden of Eden to till it and to care for it. And Jehovah gave the man this command: "You may eat all you wish from every tree of the garden, except from the tree that gives the knowledge of good and evil; from this you shall not eat, for if you eat from it you shall surely die."

Then Jehovah said, "It is not good for the man to be alone; I will make a companion for him." So out of the ground Jehovah made all the wild beasts and birds, and brought them to the man to see what he would name them; and whatever he called each living thing that became its name. But for the man himself there was found no companion suited to him.

Then Jehovah made the man fall into a deep sleep; and while he slept, he took one of his ribs and closed up its place with flesh. The rib which he had taken from the man, Jehovah made into a woman and brought her to the man. Then the man said, "Because she was made from my body, she shall be called Woman."

THE FIRST DISOBEDIENCE

Now the serpent was more deceitful than any other animal that Jehovah had made; and it said to the woman, "Has God really said, 'You shall not eat from any tree of the garden'?" The woman answered, "We may eat of the fruit of all the trees of the garden except the fruit of the tree which is in the middle of the garden, for God has said, 'You shall not eat from it, nor shall you touch it; for if you do, you shall die.'" Then the serpent said to the woman, "You shall not surely die; for God knows that as soon as you eat of it your eyes will be opened, and you will know what is good and what is evil."

When the woman saw that the tree was good for food, beautiful to look at and that it would make her wise, she took some of its fruit and ate it. Then she gave some to her husband who was with her, and he ate.

Then the eyes of both of them were opened, so that they knew that they were naked; and they sewed fig-leaves together and made girdles for themselves. When they heard the sound of the footsteps of Jehovah, as he was walking in the garden in the cool of the day, the man and his wife hid from him among the trees of the garden.

And Jehovah called to the man and said to him, "Where are you?" and he answered, "I heard the sound of thy footsteps in the garden and I was afraid, because I was naked; so I hid myself." Jehovah said, "Who told you that you were naked? Have you eaten from the tree from which I forbade you to eat?" The man answered, "The woman whom thou didst give to me--she gave me fruit from the tree and I ate." Jehovah said to the woman, "What is this that you have done?" The woman replied, "The serpent deceived me, and I ate."

Then Jehovah said to the serpent, "Because you have done this, you shall be hated more than all beasts. You shall crawl on your belly and eat dust all your life, and men and serpents shall always be enemies. They shall bruise your head, and you shall wound them on the heel."

To the woman he said, "I will greatly increase your trouble and your pain, and you shall be subject to your husband, and he shall rule over you."

But to the man he said, "Because you have listened to your wife and have eaten of the tree from which I forbade you to eat, as long as you live you shall earn a living only by hard work. By hard work shall you raise food to eat. And you shall die and your body go back to the ground, for from dust you were made, and to dust you shall return!"

And Jehovah made garments of skins for the man and his wife, and clothed them. And he sent them out of the garden of Eden to till the ground.

CAIN AND HIS BROTHER ABEL

Adam named his wife Eve, because she was the mother of all living beings. She had two sons, Cain and Abel. Abel was a shepherd, but Cainwas a farmer.

One day Cain brought, as an offering to Jehovah, some fruit and grain that he had grown. Abel, too, brought some of the best animals of his flock and sacrificed their fat pieces to Jehovah. Jehovah was pleased with Abel and his offering, but Cain and his offering did not please him.

This made Cain very angry and his face showed it. So Jehovah said to Cain, "Why are you angry and why do you scowl? If you do what is right and good, will not your offering be accepted? But if you do wrong, sin crouches like a wild beast at the door and the desire to sin will overcome you; but you should master it."

Cain said to his brother Abel, "Let us go into the field." And while they were in the field, Cain struck his brother Abel and killed him.

When Jehovah said to Cain, "Where is your brother Abel?" Cain answered, "I do not know; am I my brother's keeper?" Jehovah said, "What have you done? Hark! your brother's blood is crying to me from the ground. Even now you are condemned by the very ground that has opened to receive your brother's blood from your hand. Whenever you till the ground, it shall no longer yield to you its strength; you shall be a tramp and a wanderer on the earth."

Then Cain said to Jehovah, "My punishment is more than I can bear. See, thou hast driven me out to-day from this land, and I shall no longer be able to worship thee; I shall become a tramp and a wanderer on the earth, and whoever finds me will kill me."

But Jehovah said to him, "If any one kills you, he shall be punished sevenfold." So Jehovah placed a mark on Cain, to keep any one who found him from killing him. And Cain went out from Jehovah's presence and lived as a wanderer, away from Eden.

NOAH AND THE GREAT FLOOD

When Jehovah saw that men were growing more wicked in the world and that their thoughts were always evil, he was greatly grieved and regretted that he had made man. Therefore, Jehovah said, "I will completely destroy all living beings from off the earth, for I regret that I have made them."

But Noah had won Jehovah's favor. So Jehovah said to Noah, "I have decided to put an end to all living beings, for the earth is filled with their wicked acts. I am going to destroy them from the earth. Make yourself an ark of cypress wood. Build rooms in the ark, and cover it within and without with pitch. This is how you shall build it: the ark shall be five hundred feet long, eighty feet wide, and fifty feet high. Make a roof for it and place the door on the side. Build it with lower, second, and third stories. For I am about to bring floods of water upon the earth to destroy every living creature in which is the breath of life. Every creature that is on the earth shall die."

Then Jehovah said to Noah, "Enter with all your household into the ark, for I see that of all the people who are now alive you alone are upright. Of all the beasts that are fit for food and sacrifice you shall take with you seven, the male and the female; but of the beasts that are not fit for food and sacrifice two, the male and the female; and of the wild birds that are fit for food and sacrifice seven, to keep each kind alive on all the earth. After seven days I will send rain on the earth for forty days and forty nights; and I will destroy every living thing that I have made."

Then Noah did all that Jehovah commanded him. When the waters of the flood came upon the earth, he, his sons, his wife, and his sons' wives, together with the beasts that were fit for food and sacrifice and the beasts that were not fit, and the birds, and everything that creeps upon the ground, entered the ark because of the waters of the flood.

The rain fell upon the earth forty days and forty nights, and Jehovah shut Noah in the ark. And the waters rose higher and higher and raised up the ark, and it was lifted high above the earth. All creatures living on the land died. Noah only was left and they who were with him in the ark.

Then God remembered Noah and all the beasts and all the animals that were with him in the ark. And God caused a wind to blow over the earth, and the flood went down, the rain from heaven ceased, and the waters withdrew more and more from the land.

After forty days Noah opened the window of the ark and sent out a raven; and it kept going to and fro until the waters were dried up on the earth. He also sent out a dove to see if the waters had gone from the surface of the earth. But the dove found no rest for her foot, and so returned to him to the ark, for the waters covered the whole earth. Therefore, Noah reached out his hand and took her and brought her back into the ark.

Then he waited seven days longer and again sent out the dove from the ark. And the dove came in to him at dusk; and in her mouth was a freshly plucked olive-leaf. So Noah knew that the waters had gone from the earth. And he waited seven days more and again sent out the dove, but it did not return to him.

So Noah took off the covering of the ark and looked and saw that the surface of the ground was dry. Then he, with his sons, his wife, and his sons' wives, went out of the ark.

And Noah built an altar to Jehovah and took one of every beast and bird that was fit for sacrifice and offered burnt-offerings on the altar. And Jehovah said to himself, "I will never again condemn the ground because of man, nor will I again destroy every living creature, as I have done. While the earth remains, seedtime and harvest, cold and heat, summer and winter, day and night, shall not cease."

And God said, "This is the sign of the solemn agreement that I make for all time between me and you and every living creature that is with you: I have placed my rainbow in the cloud and it shall be the sign of the solemn agreement between me and the people who live on the earth. Whenever I bring a cloud over the earth and the rainbow is seen in the cloud, I will remember the agreement which is between me and you and every living creature; and the waters shall never again become a flood to destroy them."

THE STORY OF THE TOWER OF BABEL

All the people of the earth spoke one language; and as they travelled westward, they found a broad valley in the land of Babylonia, and made their home there.

Then they said one to another, "Come, let us make bricks and thoroughly bake them." So they had bricks for stone and asphalt for mortar. And they said, "Come, let us build us a city, and a tower whose top will touch the heavens, and thus make a landmark, that we may not be scattered over all the earth."

But when Jehovah came down to see the city and the tower men had built, he said, "See, they are one people and all have one language. This is but the beginning, and now nothing which they plan to do will seem too difficult for them. Come, let us go down and confuse their language, that they may not understand one another."

So Jehovah scattered them from there over all the earth; and they stopped building the city. Therefore they named it Babel, which means Confusion, for there Jehovah confused the language of all the people on the earth and scattered them over the whole world.

ABRAHAM, THE FRIEND OF GOD AND MAN

The sons of Noah who came out of the ark were Shem, Ham and Japheth. Terah, a descendant of Shem, was the father of Abraham, Nahor and Haran; and Haran was the father of Lot.

Jehovah said to Abraham, "Go from your country, your relatives, and your father's house to the land that I will show you. And I will make of you a great nation; and I will surely bless you and make your name famous, so that you shall be a blessing. And all the families of the earth shall ask for themselves a blessing like your own."

So Abraham set out, as Jehovah had commanded him; and Lot went with him. Abraham was seventy-five years old when he left Haran. He took Sarah his wife and Lot his brother's son and everything that they had, and started for the land of Canaan.

Abraham passed through the land to a place called Shechem, to the oak of Moreh. There Jehovah appeared to Abraham and said, "To your children will I give this land." There Abraham built an altar to Jehovah who had appeared to him. From there he removed to the hill near Bethel and pitched his tent with Bethel on one side and Ai on the other, and there too he built an altar to Jehovah and prayed to him.

Now Abraham was very rich in cattle, in silver, and in gold; Lot also, who went with Abraham, had so many flocks and herds and tents that the land was not rich enough to support them both. So when there was a quarrel between Lot's herdsmen and Abraham's herdsmen, Abraham said to Lot, "I beg of you, let there be no quarrel between me and you, nor between my herdsmen and yours, for we are relatives. Is not the whole land before you? I beg of you, separate yourself from me. If you go to the left, then I will go to the right; or if you go to the right, then I will go to the left."

So Lot looked about and saw that all the plain of the Jordan, as far as Zoar, was well watered everywhere, like a garden of Jehovah. So Lot chose for himself all the valley of the Jordan, and lived in the cities of the plain and moved his tent as far as Sodom. But the men of Sodom were very wicked and sinned against Jehovah.

Jehovah said to Abraham, after Lot had gone away from him, "Lift up your eyes and look from the place where you are northward, southward, eastward and westward, for all the land that you see I will give to you and to your children forever. I will make them as many as the dust of the earth, so that if a man can count the dust of the earth, then your children may also be counted. Rise, walk through the length and breadth of the land, for I will give it to you."

Then Abraham moved his tent and lived in the oak grove of Mamre, which is in Hebron, and built there an altar to Jehovah.

Jehovah also appeared to Abraham by the oaks of Mamre, as he was sitting at the entrance of his tent in the heat of the day; and, as he looked up, three men stood there before him. As soon as he saw them, he ran from the e ntrance of his tent to meet them and bowed to the ground and said, "Sirs, if you are willing to do me a favor, do not, I beg of you, pass by your servant. Since you have come to your servant, let a little water be brought, that you may wash your feet, and lie down under thetree. And let me bring some food, that you may refresh yourselves; afterward you may go on your way." They replied, "Do as you have said."

So Abraham hastened to Sarah's tent and said, "Make ready quickly four measures of fine meal, knead it, and make cakes." Abraham also ran to the herd, and took a calf that was tender and good, and gave it to the servant, and he prepared it quickly. Then Abraham took curd and milk, with the calf which he had prepared, and served them; and he waited on them under the tree, while they ate.

Then they said to him, "Where is your wife?" He said, "There, within the tent." One of them said, "I will surely return to you about nine monthsfrom now, and then, Sarah your wife shall have a son."

LOT'S ESCAPE FROM A WICKED CITY

And Abraham went along with them to start them on their way. Jehovah said, "The complaint has come that the people of Sodom and Gomorrah have committed great and terrible sins. I will go down and see whether they have done exactly as the complaint comes to me; and if they have not, I will know."

Then the men turned from there and looked off in the direction of Sodom.

Then Abraham drew near to Jehovah and said, "Wilt thou sweep away the righteous with the wicked? Suppose there are within the city fiftypeople who are righteous. Wilt thou sweep away and not spare the place for the fifty righteous who are in it? Far be it from thee to do this: to slay the righteous with the wicked! And that the righteous should be treated as the wicked, far be it from thee! Shall not the Judge of all the earth do what is just?" Jehovah said, "If I find in the city of Sodom fifty who are righteous, I will spare the whole place for their sake." Abraham answered, "I have dared to speak to Jehovah, even though I am but dust and ashes. Suppose there be five lacking of the fifty righteous. Wilt thou sweep away all the city for lack of five?" Jehovah said, "I will not sweep it away, if I find forty-five there."

Then Abraham spoke to him again, and said, "Suppose forty are found there?" He replied, "For the sake of forty I will not do it." Then Abraham said, "Oh, let not Jehovah be angry, but let me speak. Suppose thirty are found there?" He answered, "I will not do it, if I find thirty there." Then Abraham said, "Thou seest that I have dared to speak to Jehovah. Suppose twenty are found there?" He replied, "For the sake of twenty I will not destroy it." Then Abraham said, "Oh, let not Jehovah be angry, but let me speak just once more. Suppose ten are found there?" And he said, "For the sake of the ten I will not destroy it." Then Jehovah went his way, and Abraham returned home.

Two angels in human form came to Sodom in the evening, as Lot was sitting at the gate of Sodom. When Lot saw them, he rose up to meet them, and he bowed with his face to the earth and said, "Sirs, turn aside, I beg of you, into your servant's house and spend the night and wash your feet; then you can rise up early and go on your way." They said, "No, we will spend the night in the street." But he urged them so strongly that they went with him and entered his house. And he made a feast for them and baked bread made without yeast, and they ate.

But before they had lain down, the people of Sodom, both young and old, all the people from every quarter, surrounded the house. And they called out to Lot, "Where are the men who came in to you to-night? Bring them out to us that we may do to them what we desire."

Then Lot went out to them at the entrance of his house, but he shut the door after him. And he said, "I beg of you, my friends, do not do what is wrong. Do nothing to these men, for they have come under the shadow of my roof." But they replied, "Stand back, or we will treat you worse than them." And they pressed hard against Lot and advanced to break the door. But the men reached out and drew Lot to them into the house and shut the door. Then they smote the men who were at the door of the house, both small and great, with blindness, so that they grew tired of searching for the door.

Then the men said to Lot, "Have you any one else here? Bring your sons-in-law, your sons, and daughters, and whoever you have in the city out of this place, for we are about to destroy it, because great complaint concerning the people has come to Jehovah and he has sent us to destroy it." So Lot went out and said to his sons-in-law, "Up, go out of this place, for Jehovah will destroy the city." But his sons-in-law thought he was only jesting.

When the dawn appeared, the angels urged Lot, saying, "Get up, take your wife and your two daughters that you may not be swept away in the punishment of the city." When he hesitated, the men took him by the hand and led him and his wife and his two daughters outside the city, for Jehovah was merciful to him.

When they had brought them outside, they said, "Run for your life; do not look behind you nor stay anywhere in the plain. Escape to the heights, that you may not be swept away!" But Lot said to them, "Oh, sirs, not so! See, your servant has found favor with you, and you have shown great mercy to me in saving my life. I cannot escape to the heights, lest some evil overtake me, and I die. See now, this village is near enough to run to, and it is small. Oh, let me escape there, and my life will be saved." Jehovah said to him, "I have also granted you this favor, in that I will not destroy the village of which you have spoken. Make haste, escape to it, for I can do nothing until you arrive there."

The sun had risen when Lot came to Zoar. Then Jehovah caused brimstone and fire from heaven to rain upon Sodom and Gomorrah, and he destroyed those cities and all the plain, with all the people who lived in it and all that grew on the ground. But Lot's wife, who was following him, looked back, and she became a pillar of salt.

Early in the morning Abraham rose and went to the place where he had stood before Jehovah; and as he looked toward Sodom and Gomorrah and all the plain, he saw the smoke of the land going up as the smoke of a smelting-furnace.

GOD'S CARE FOR THE BOY ISHMAEL

Jehovah remembered what he had told Sarah, and he did as he had promised. So Sarah had a son, and when the child grew up, Abraham made a great feast on the day that he was weaned. But Sarah saw the son of Hagar the Egyptian and of Abraham playing with her son Isaac. And she said to Abraham, "Drive out this slave girl and her son, for the son of this slave girl shall not be heir with my son Isaac." This request was very displeasing to Abraham because the boy was his son. But Jehovah said to Abraham, "Do not be displeased because of the boy and because of your slave girl. Listen to all that Sarah says to you, for Isaac only and his children shall bear your name. But I will also make of the son of the slave girl a great nation, because he is your son."

Then Abraham rose early in the morning and took bread and a skin of water and gave it to Hagar; and he put the boy upon her shoulder and sent her away. So she set out and wandered in the desert of Beersheba. When the water in the skin was gone, she left the child under one of the desert shrubs and went a short distance away and sat down opposite him, for she said, "Let me not see the child die."

While she sat there, the boy began to cry; and Jehovah heard the cry of the boy, and said, "What troubles you, Hagar? Fear not, for Jehovah has heard the cry of the boy. Rise, lift him up, and hold him fast by the hand, for I will make him a great nation." And Jehovah opened her eyes and she saw a well of water. Then she went and filled the skin with water and gave the boy a drink.

And Jehovah cared for the boy; and when he grew up, he lived in the wilderness of Paran and became a bowman. And his mother secured a wife for him from Egypt.

ABRAHAM'S LOYALTY TO GOD

Later Jehovah tested Abraham, saying to him, "Abraham"; and he answered, "Here am I." Jehovah said, "Take your son, your only son Isaac, whom you love, and go to the land of Moriah, and offer him there as a burnt-offering on one of the mountains of which I shall tell you."

So Abraham rose early in the morning and saddled his ass and took two of his servants with him, and his son Isaac. When he had split the wood for the burnt-offering, he set out for the place of which God had told him. On the third day, when Abraham looked up and saw the place in the distance, he said to his servants, "Stay here with the ass, while I and the lad go over there. When we have worshipped, we will come back to you."

Then Abraham took the wood for the burnt-offering and laid it on Isaac, his son. And he took the fire and the knife, and they both went on together. And Isaac spoke to Abraham his father and said, "My father!" and Abraham answered, "Yes, my son." Isaac said, "Here is the fire and the wood, but where is the lamb for a burnt-offering?" Abraham answered, "My son, God will himself provide a lamb for a burnt-offering." So the two went on together.

When they came to the place of which God had told him, Abraham built the altar there and laid the wood on it and bound Isaac his son and laid him on the altar upon the wood. Then Abraham reached out his hand, and took the knife to kill his son. But the angel of Jehovah called to him from heaven, saying, "Abraham, Abraham!" and he answered, "Here am I." And he said, "Do not put your hand upon the boy, nor do anything to him, for now I know that you love God, for you have not refused to give your son, your only son, to him."

Then Abraham looked up, and he saw a ram caught in the thicket by his horns. So Abraham took the ram and offered him up as a burnt-offering instead of his son. And he named the place Jehovah-jireh, which means, "Jehovah will Provide."

The angel of Jehovah again called to Abraham and said, "Jehovah declares, 'Because you have done this thing and have not kept back your son, your only son, I will surely bless you, and I will make your children as many as the stars of the heavens and as the sand, which is on the seashore, so that they shall conquer their enemies, and all the nations of the earth shall ask for themselves a blessing like theirs, because you have obeyed my command.'"

HOW REBEKAH BECAME THE WIFE OF ISAAC

When Abraham was very old and Jehovah had blessed him in every way, Abraham said to the eldest of his household servants, who had charge of all his affairs, "Put your hand under my hip, while I make you promise by Jehovah, the God of heaven and earth, that you will not let my son marry one of the daughters of the Canaanites, among whom I live, but that you will go to my own country and to my relatives and there get a wife for my son Isaac." The servant said to him, "Perhaps the woman will not be willing to follow me to this land. Must I then take your son back to the land from which you came?" Abraham said to him, "See to it that you do not take my son back there. Jehovah, the God of heaven, who took me from my father's house and from my native land and who solemnly promised me, 'To your children I will give this land,' will send his angel before you and there you will get a wife for my son. But if the woman is not willing to come with you, then you will be free from this promise to me; only never take my son back there." So the servant put his hand under Abraham's hip and made the promise.

Then the servant took ten of his master's camels and set out with precious gifts from his master. So he went to the town of Nahor. And he made the camels kneel down outside the town by the well in the evening, at the time when women go out to draw water. Then he said, "O Jehovah, the God of my master Abraham, give me, I pray thee, success to-day, and show kindness to my master Abraham. Here I am standing by the spring of water, and the daughters of the men of the town are coming out to draw water. May that young woman to whom I shall say, 'Please let down your water-jar that I may drink'; and who answers, 'Drink and I will also water your camels,' may she be the one thou hast chosen for thy servant

Isaac. By this I shall know that thou hast shown kindness to my master."

Then even before he was through speaking, Rebekah, who was the grand-daughter of Nahor, Abraham's brother, came out with her water-jar upon her shoulder. She was very beautiful and unmarried. She went down to the spring, filled her jar, and came up. Then the servant ran to meet her and said, "Please let me drink a little water from your jar." She answered, "Drink, sir," and quickly let down her water-jar from her shoulder upon her hand and gave him a drink.

When she had finished giving him a drink she said, "I will draw water for your camels also, until they have finished drinking." So she quickly emptied her jar into the trough and ran again to the well to draw water, and drew for all his camels. Meanwhile the man was silently gazing at her in order to find out whether Jehovah had made his journey successful or not.

As soon as the camels had finished drinking, the man took a gold ring, five ounces in weight, and put it in her nose, and put on her arms two golden bracelets weighing five ounces, and said, "Whose daughter are you? Tell me, I beg of you. Is there room in your father's house for us to spend the night?" She answered, "I am the grand-daughter of Milcah and Nahor. We have plenty of straw and feed, and there is a place for you to spend the night."

Then the man bowed his head and worshipped Jehovah, saying, "Blessed be Jehovah, the God of my master Abraham, who has continued to show his mercy and his faithfulness toward my master. As for me, Jehovah has led me on the way to the house of my master's relatives."

Then the young woman ran and told these things to her mother's family. Now Rebekah had a brother named Laban; and Laban ran out to the man at the spring. And when he saw the bracelets on his sister's hands and the ring, and when he heard Rebekah say, "This is what the man said to me," he went to the man, who was still standing by the camels at the spring, and said, "Come in, you who are blessed by Jehovah! Why do you stand outside? For I have cleared the house and have room for the camels." So he brought the man into the house and took the packs off the camels and furnished straw and feed for them, and water to wash his feet and the feet of the men who were with him.

But when food was set before him to eat, he said, "I will not eat until I have made known my errand." They answered, "Speak." He said, "I am Abraham's servant; and Jehovah has blessed my master greatly, so that he has become very rich. He has given him flocks and herds, silver and gold, servants, and camels and asses. Now Sarah, my master's wife, had a son when she was old, and my master has given him all that he has. My master also made me promise, saying, 'Do not let my son marry one of the daughters of the Canaanites, in whose land I live, but go to my father's home and to my relatives and there find a wife for my son.'

"When I said to my master, 'What if the woman will not follow me?' he said to me, 'Jehovah, whom I love and serve, will send his angel with you and make you successful, and you will find for my son a wife from among my relatives and my father's family. Then you shall be free from your promise to me. But if you go to my family and they do not give her to you, you shall also be free from your promise to me.' So I came to-day to the spring and said, 'O Jehovah, the God of my master Abraham, see, I am standing by the spring of water, if thou wilt make the errand on which I am going successful, then let the young woman who comes to draw, to whom I say, Please give me a little water from your jar to drink, and who shall say to me, Drink, and I will also draw for your camels, let that one be the woman whom Jehovah has chosen for my master's son.'

"Even before I was through speaking, Rebekah came out with her water-jar on her shoulder and went down to the spring and drew water. And when I said to her, 'Please let me drink,' she quickly let down her water-jar from her shoulder and answered, 'Drink, and I will also water your camels.' So I drank, and she also watered the camels. Then I asked her, 'Whose daughter are you?' And she said, 'The grand-daughter of Nahor and Milcah.' So I put the ring in her nose and the bracelets on her arms. And I bowed my head and worshipped and blessed Jehovah the God of my master Abraham who had led me on the right way to find the daughter of my master's brother for his son. Tell me whether or not you will deal kindly and truly with my master, so that I shall know what to do!"

Then Laban and his family answered, "The matter is in the hands of Jehovah. We cannot say either 'yes' or 'no.' See, Rebekah is before you; take her and go and let her be the wife of your master's son, as Jehovah has said."

When Abraham's servant heard their words, he bowed to the ground before Jehovah. Then he brought out gold and silver ornaments and clothing and gave them to Rebekah. He also gave costly gifts to her brother and to her mother. And he and the men who were with him ate and drank and spent the night there.

When they rose in the morning, the servant said, "Send me away to my master." But Rebekah's brother and mother answered, "Let the young woman stay with us a month or at least ten days; after that she may go." But he said to them, "Do not delay me, for Jehovah has given me success.Send me away that I may go to my master."

Then they said, "We will call the young woman and ask her." So they called Rebekah and said to her, "Will you go with this man?" She answered, "I will go." So they sent away their sister Rebekah and her nurse with Abraham's servant and his men.

They also blessed Rebekah, saying to her, "Our sister! may your children and their children become thousands and thousands!" Then Rebekah set out with her maids and, riding upon the camels, they followed the man. So the servant took Rebekah and went away.

Now Abraham had given all that he had to Isaac and had breathed his last, dying in a good old age, satisfied with living. In the evening, when Isaac had gone out in the field to meditate, he looked up and saw camels coming. Rebekah too looked up, and when she saw Isaac, she quickly alighted from the camel and said to the servant, "Who is this man walking in the field to meet us?" When the servant said, "It is my master," she took her veil and covered her face. Then the servant told Isaac all that he had done. And Isaac brought Rebekah to the tent of Sarah his mother, and she became his wife; and he loved her.

HOW JACOB DECEIVED HIS FATHER

Now Isaac prayed to Jehovah for his wife, because she had no children; and Jehovah heard his prayer, and Rebekah became the mother of twin boys. They named one Esau and the other Jacob.

As they grew up, Esau became a skilful hunter, a man who lived out in the fields; but Jacob was a quiet man who stayed about the tents. Isaac loved Esau, for he was fond of game; but Rebekah loved Jacob.

Once when Jacob was preparing a stew, Esau came in from the fields, and he was very hungry; so he said to Jacob, "Let me swallow some of that red stew, for I am very hungry." But Jacob said, "Sell me first of all your right as the eldest." Esau replied, "See, I am nearly dead now! So of what use is this birthright to me?" Jacob said, "First solemnly promise to give it to me." So Esau solemnly promised and sold his birthright to Jacob. Then Jacob gave Esau bread and stewed lentils, and when he had had something to eat and drink, he got up and went away. In this way Esau gave away his birthright.

When Isaac was so old and so nearly blind that he could not see, he called Esau his oldest son and said to him, "My son." Esau answered, "Here am I." Then Isaac said, "See, I am old and do not know how soon I may die. Now, therefore, take your quiver and your bow and go out into the fields and hunt game for me and prepare for me savory food, such as I love, and bring it to me that I may eat and that I may bless you before I die."

Rebekah was listening when Isaac spoke to his son Esau. So when Esau went into the fields to hunt game, Rebekah said to her son Jacob, "I just now heard your father say to your brother Esau, 'Bring me game and prepare for me savory food that I may eat it and bless you before I die.' Now, my son, do as I tell you: Go to the flock and bring me from there two good kids, and I will make of them savory food for your father, such as he loves. Then take it to him, that he may eat, so that he may bless you before he dies." But Jacob said to Rebekah his mother, "You know that my brother Esau is a hairy man, while I am smooth. Perhaps my father will feel of me; then I shall appear to him as a deceiver, and I shall bring blame upon me and not a blessing." But his mother said to him, "Upon me be the blame, my son; only obey me and go, bring the kids to me." So he went and brought them to his mother, and his mother made savory food such as his father loved.

Rebekah also took the fine clothes of her older son Esau, which she had with her in the tent, and put them on her younger son Jacob. Then she put the skins of the kids upon his hands and upon the smooth part of his neck, and she placed the savory food and the bread which she had prepared in his hand, and he went to his father and said, "My father." Isaac answered, "Here am I; who are you, my son?" Jacob said, "I am Esau your oldest son. I have done as you commanded me. Sit up and eat of my game, that you may bless me." Isaac said to his son, "How very quickly you have found it, my son." He answered, "Yes, because Jehovah your God gave me success."

Then Isaac said to Jacob, "Come here, my son, that I may feel of you to find out whether you are really my son Esau or not." So Jacob went near to Isaac his father, and he felt of him and said, "The voice is the voice of Jacob, but the hands are the hands of Esau. Are you really myson Esau?" Jacob answered, "I am." And Isaac did not recognize him, for his hands were hairy like his brother Esau's. So he blessed him. Then Isaac said, "Bring the food to me, that I may eat of my son's game and bless you." So he brought it to him, and he ate. Jacob also brought him wine, and he drank.

Then his father Isaac said to him, "Come near now and kiss me, my son." As he came near and kissed him, he smelled the smell of his garment, and blessed him.

As soon as Isaac had given Jacob his blessing, and Jacob was about to leave his father, Esau his brother came in from his hunting. He also had made savory food and was bringing it to his father. So he said to him, "Father, rise and eat of your son's game, that you may bless me." But Isaac his father said to him, "Who are you?" He answered, "I am your son, your oldest, Esau." Then Isaac trembled and said, "Who then is he that has hunted game and brought it to me, so that I ate plentifully before you came, and blessed him? Also blessed shall he be!"

When Esau heard the words of his father, he uttered a loud and bitter cry and said to his father, "Bless me, even me also, O my father."

But Isaac said, "Your brother came with deceit and has taken away your blessing." Esau said, "Is it not because he was named Jacob, which means Supplanter, that he has supplanted me these two times: he took my birthright, and now he has taken my blessing!" Then he said, "Have you kept a blessing for me?" Isaac answered Esau, "See, I have made him your master and I have given to him all his relatives as servants and grain and wine as his food. What then can I do for you, my son?" Esau said to his father, "Is that the only blessing you have, my father?" and Esau began to weep aloud. Then Isaac his father answered him:

"You shall live far from earth's fertile places,
And away from the dew of heaven.
By your sword you shall live,
And your brother you shall serve."

JACOB'S DREAM

Esau hated Jacob because of the blessing which his father had given him. And Esau said to himself, "My father will soon die; then I will kill Jacob, my brother."

When the words of her older son Esau were told to Rebekah, she sent for her younger son Jacob and said to him, "Your brother, Esau, is going to kill you. Now therefore, my son, listen to me: run away to my brother Laban at Haran and stay with him for a time until your brother is no longer angry and he forgets what you have done to him. Then I will send and bring you back. Why should I lose both of you in one day?"

Then Jacob set out from Beersheba and went toward Haran. And when he arrived at a certain place, he passed the night there, because the sun had set. And he took one of the stones from its place and put it under his head and lay down to sleep. Then he dreamed and saw a ladder set up on the earth, and its top reached to heaven; and the angels of God were going up and down on it.

Jehovah also stood beside him and said, "I am Jehovah, the God of Abraham and the God of Isaac. The land on which you lie I will give to you and to your children. See, I am with you, and will keep you wherever you go and will bring you again to this land; for I will not leave you until I have done what I have promised you."

When Jacob awoke from his sleep, he said, "Surely Jehovah is in this place, and I did not know it." And he was filled with awe and said, "This place is the house of God, and this is the gate of heaven."

So Jacob rose early in the morning and took the stone that he had put under his head and set it up as a pillar and poured oil upon the top of it. And he named that place Bethel, which means House of God. Jacob also made this promise, "If God will be with me and protect me on this journey which I am making and give me bread to eat and clothing to put on, and if I return safe and sound to my father's house, then Jehovah shall be my God, and this stone which I have set up as a pillar shall be a house of God. And of all that thou shalt give me I will surely give a tenth to thee."

THE DECEIVER DECEIVED

Then Jacob went on his journey and arrived at the land of the children of the East. And he looked and saw a well in the field, and there were three flocks of sheep lying down by it; for from that well they watered the flocks; but there was a large stone over the well. When all the flocks were gathered there, they used to roll away the stone and water the sheep and then put the stone back in its place over the well.

Jacob said to the men, "My friends, from where do you come?" They said, "We are from Haran." Then he said to them, "Do you know Laban the son of Nahor?" And they said, "We know him." And he said to them, "Is all well with him?" And they said, "All is well; indeed, this is Rachel his daughter coming with the sheep." And he said, "See, the sun is still high! It is not time for the cattle to be gathered together. Water the sheep and feed them." But they said, "We cannot until all the flocks are gathered together, and they roll away the stone from the well; then we will water the sheep."

While he was still speaking with them, Rachel came with her father's sheep; for she was a shepherdess. When Jacob saw Rachel the daughter of Laban, his mother's brother, and Laban's sheep, he went up and rolled the stone from the well and watered the flock of Laban his mother's brother. Then Jacob kissed Rachel and wept aloud. And when Jacob told Rachel that he was a relative of her father and that he was Rebekah's son, she ran and told her father.

As soon as Laban heard about Jacob, his sister's son, he ran to meet him, put his arms around him, kissed him many times, and brought him to his home. When

Jacob told Laban all about these things, Laban said to him, "Surely you are my bone and my flesh." So he remained with him a whole month.

Then Laban said to Jacob, "Should you serve me for nothing simply because you are related to me? Tell me what shall be your wages?" Now Laban had two daughters: the name of the older was Leah, and the name of the younger was Rachel. Leah's eyes were weak, but Rachel was beautiful. Jacob loved Rachel, and so he said, "I will serve you seven years for Rachel your younger daughter." And Laban said, "It is better for me to give her to you than to give her to any other man. Stay with me." So Jacob served seven years for Rachel, and they seemed to him but a few days, because he loved her so.

Then Jacob said to Laban, "Give me my wife, for my time is up, and let me marry her." So Laban gathered all the men of the place and made a feast. In the evening he took Leah his daughter and brought her to him, and Jacob received her as his wife.

When in the morning Jacob found it was Leah, he said to Laban, "What is this you have done to me? Did I not serve you for Rachel? Why then have you deceived me?" Laban said, "It is not the custom among us to give the younger in marriage before the older. Remain with this one during the marriage week, then we will give you the other also for the service which you shall give me during seven more years." Jacob did so: he remained with Leah during the marriage week. Then Laban gave him Rachel his daughter to be his wife, but Jacob loved Rachel more than Leah. So he had to serve Laban seven years more.

MEETING A BROTHER WHO HAD BEEN WRONGED

In time Jacob became very wealthy, and he had large flocks, slaves, and asses. But he heard Laban's sons say, "Jacob has taken all that was our father's, and from that which was our father's he has gotten all this wealth." He also saw that Laban did not act toward him the same as before. So Jacob rose and put his sons and his wives upon the camels and drove away all his cattle. He deceived Laban, for he did not tell him that he was fleeing away. So he fled across the river Euphrates, with all that he had, and set out on his way toward Mount Gilead.

Then Jacob sent messengers before him to his brother Esau. And he gave them this command, "Say to my lord Esau: 'Your servant Jacob declares, I have lived with Laban and have stayed until now. I have oxen and asses, flocks and slaves, and I have sent to tell my lord, in order that I may win your favor.'" The messengers returned to Jacob with the report, "We came to your brother Esau, even as he was coming to meet you with four hundred men."

Then Jacob was greatly alarmed and worried. So he divided the people that were with him and the flocks and the herds and the camels into two parts and said, "If Esau comes to the one and attacks and destroys it, then the other which is left can escape."

Jacob also prayed, "O God of my father Abraham and God of my father Isaac, deliver me, I pray thee, from the hand of my brother, from the hand of Esau, for I fear that he will come and attack me and kill the mothers and the children."

Then Jacob took as a present for his brother Esau, two hundred female goats and twenty male goats, two hundred ewes and twenty rams, thirty milch camels and their young, forty cows and ten bulls, twenty female asses and ten young asses. These he put, each drove by itself, in the care of his servants and said to them, "Go on before me and leave a space between the droves."

He gave those in front this command: "When my brother Esau meets you and asks you, 'To whom do you belong? and where are you going? and whose are these before you?' then you shall say, 'To your servant Jacob; it is a present sent by him to my lord Esau; and Jacob himself is just behind us.'" Jacob also commanded the second, and the third, and all that followed the droves, to make the same answer, and to say, "Jacob himself is just behind us." For he said to himself, "I will please him with the present that goes before me, and then, when I meet him, perhaps he will welcome me." So he sent the present over before him; but he himself spent that night in the camp.

Later that night he rose up and took his two wives, his two maid servants, and his eleven children, and sent them over the river Jabbok.

Jacob was left alone, and one wrestled with him until daybreak. When he saw that he did not win against Jacob, he struck the socket of his hip, and the socket of Jacob's hip was strained, as he wrestled with him. Then he said, "Let me go, for the dawn is breaking." But Jacob replied, "I will not let thee go unless you bless me." So he said to him, "What is your name?" He answered, "Jacob." Then he said, "Your name shall be no longer Jacob, but Israel, which means Struggler with God; for you have struggled with God and with men and have won." So he blessed him there. And Jacob called the place Penuel, which means Face of God, for he said, "I have seen God face to face, and my life has been saved."

When Jacob looked up, he saw Esau coming with four hundred men. And he put the maid servants and their children in front, Leah and her children next, and Rachel and her son Joseph in the rear. Then Jacob himself went in front of them, and he bowed down to the ground seven times, as he drew near to his brother. Esau ran to meet him, threw his arms about his neck, and kissed him, and they wept.

When Esau looked up and saw the women and the children, he said, "Who are these with you?" Jacob answered, "The children whom God has so kindly given me." Then the maid servants with their children came up and bowed down to the ground. Leah and her children also came and bowed down, and afterward Joseph and Rachel came up and bowed down before Esau.

Esau asked, "What do you mean by all this company which I met?" Jacob answered, "To win your friendship, my lord." Esau said, "I have enough, my brother; keep what you have." But Jacob replied, "No, if now I have won your favor, receive this present from me to show that you are my friend. Take, I beg of you, the gift that I bring to you, for God has been generous to me, and I have enough." So he urged Esau until he took it.

Then Esau said, "Let me at least leave with you some of the people who are with me." But Jacob replied, "What need is there? Let me only enjoy your friendship, my Lord." So Esau turned back that day on his way to Seir.

JOSEPH SOLD AS A SLAVE BY HIS BROTHERS

When Joseph was seventeen years old, he and his brothers were shepherds, but he made them angry, for he brought a bad report about them to their father. Now Jacob loved his son Joseph, who was born in his old age; and he made him a long coat with sleeves. When his brothers saw that their father loved him more than all his other sons, they hated Joseph and would not speak to him in a friendly way.

Joseph had a dream which he told to his brothers; and they hated him still more. This is what he said to them, "I dreamed that, as we were binding sheaves in the field, my sheaf rose up and remained standing, while your sheaves came around and bowed down to my sheaf." His brothers said to him, "Will you really be king over us? Will you indeed rule over us?" So they hated him still more because of his dreams and his words.

Then he had another dream and told it to his brothers, saying, "I have had another dream, and it seemed to me that the sun and the moon and eleven stars bowed down to me." But when he told it to his father and his brothers, his father reproved him and said, "What is this dream that you have dreamed? Shall I and your mother and your brothers indeed come and bow down to the earth before you?" Therefore his brothers were jealous of him; but his father remembered the dream.

When his brothers went to pasture his father's flocks in Shechem, Jacob said to Joseph, "Go, see whether all goes well with your brothers and with the flock, and bring me back word." So he sent him out, and a certain man found him, as he was wandering in the field, and the man asked him, "What are you looking for?" He said, "I am looking for my brothers; tell me, I beg of you, where they are pasturing the flock."

The man said, "They have gone away, for I heard them say, 'Let us go to Dothan.'" So Joseph went after his brothers and found them in Dothan.

When they saw him in the distance, before he came to them, they planned together to kill him. And they said one to another, "See, here comes that great dreamer! Come, let us kill him and throw him into one of the pits, and we will say, 'A fierce beast has devoured him.' Then we shall see what will become of his dreams!"

Judah, however, when he heard it, saved Joseph's life by saying, "Let us not take his life." Reuben also said to them, "Do not shed blood; throw him into this pit, here in the wilderness; but do not harm him." Reuben said this to save Joseph from their hands so that he could bring him back to his father. So when Joseph came to his brothers, they took off his long coat with sleeves and threw him into the pit. But the pit was empty, there being no water in it.

Then they sat down to eat and, when they looked up, they saw a band of Ishmaelites coming from Gilead; and their camels were loaded with spices, gum, and ladanum on their way to carry it down to Egypt. And Judah said to his brothers, "What do we gain if we kill our brother and hide his blood? Come, let us sell him to the Ishmaelites, and let us do him no harm, for he is our brother, our own flesh and blood." So his brothers listened to him; and, drawing up Joseph, they sold him for twenty pieces of silver to the Ishmaelites, who brought him to Egypt.

Then his brothers took Joseph's long coat, killed a he-goat, dipped the coat in the blood, and brought it to their father, and said, "We found this; see whether it is your son's coat or not." He recognized it and said, "It is my son's coat! A wild beast has devoured him! Joseph surely is torn in pieces." Then Jacob tore his clothes, put sackcloth about his waist, and mourned for his son many days. All his sons and his daughters tried to comfort him, but he refused to be comforted, saying, "I shall go down to the grave mourning for my son." Thus Joseph's father mourned for him.

JOSEPH'S EAGERNESS TO HELP OTHERS

Joseph was taken down to Egypt, and Potiphar, an Egyptian, one of Pharaoh's officers, the captain of the guard, bought him from the Ishmaelites.

Now Jehovah was with Joseph, so that he prospered; and he was in the house of his master, the Egyptian. When his master saw that Jehovah was with him and made everything succeed that he undertook, he trusted him and made him his own servant. He also made him overseer of his household and placed all that he had in his care. From the time that he made him overseer in his house and over all that he had, Jehovah blessed the Egyptian's household for Joseph's sake, and the blessing of Jehovah was upon all that he had in the house and in the field. Potiphar left all that he had in Joseph's charge, and he knew nothing about his affairs except about the food which he ate. And Joseph was handsome and attractive.

After these honors had come to Joseph, his master's wife tried to tempt him to be unfaithful to his trust. But he refused, saying to her, "See, my master knows nothing about what I do in the house, and he has put all that he has in my charge. How then can I do this great wrong and sin against God?" Day after day she tempted Joseph, but he did not listen to her. One day, however, when he went into the house to do his work and when none of the men of the household were at home, she caught hold of his garment and again tried to tempt him, but he left his garment in her hand and fled out of the house.

She kept his garment by her until his master came home; then she said to him, "The Hebrew slave whom you have brought to us came to me to insult me; and when I cried aloud, he left his garment with me and fled."

When Joseph's master heard what his wife said to him, he was very angry; and he took Joseph and put him into the prison, in the place where the king's prisoners were kept. So he was left there in prison. But Jehovah was with Joseph and showed kindness to him and helped him to win the friendship of the keeper of the prison, so that he placed all the prisoners in Joseph's charge and made him responsible for whatever they did there.

After these things the butler of the king of Egypt and his baker offended their master the king of Egypt, and Pharaoh was so angry with these two officers that he put them in the same prison where Joseph was. And the captain of the guard appointed Joseph to wait on them; and they stayed in prison for some time.

And the butler and the baker of the king of Egypt, who were in the prison, both had dreams the same night, each with a different meaning. When Joseph came in to them in the morning, he saw plainly that they were sad. So he asked Pharaoh's officers, "Why do you look so sad to-day?" They answered, "We have had a dream, and there is no one who can tell what it means." Then Joseph said to them, "Is not God the one who knows what dreams mean? Tell them to me, if you will."

Then the chief butler told his dream to Joseph and said to him, "In my dream I saw a vine before me, and on the vine were three branches, and the buds put out blossoms, and its clusters brought forth ripe grapes. Pharaoh's cup was in my hand,

and I took the grapes and squeezed the juice into his cup and gave the cup to Pharaoh."

Then Joseph said to him, "This is what it means: the three branches are three days. Within three days Pharaoh will let you out of prison and restore you to your office, and you will give Pharaoh's cup into his hand as you used to do when you were his butler. But when all goes well with you, remember me, show kindness to me and speak for me to Pharaoh and bring me out of this prison; for I was unjustly stolen from the land of the Hebrews, and here also I have done nothing that they should put me in the dungeon."

When the chief baker saw that the meaning of the butler's dream was good, he said to Joseph, "I also saw something in my dream: there were three baskets of white bread on my head, and in the upper basket there were all kinds of baked food for Pharaoh, and the birds were eating them out of the basket on my head." Joseph answered, "This is what it means: the three baskets are three days; within three days Pharaoh will take off your head and hang you on a tree, and the birds shall eat your flesh."

Now on the third day, which was Pharaoh's birthday, he made a feast for all his servants. Then he set free the chief butler and the chief baker. He restored the chief butler to his office, so that he again gave the cup to Pharaoh; but the chief baker he hanged, as Joseph had told them. Yet the chief butler did not remember Joseph, but forgot him.

A PRISONER WHO BECAME A MIGHTY RULER

Two years later Pharaoh had a dream: as he stood by the river Nile, he saw coming up from the water seven cows, well fed and fat, for they had been feeding in the river grass. Then seven other cows came up after them out of the Nile, poorly fed and thin, and they stood by the other cows on the bank of the Nile. The poorly fed, lean cows ate up the seven well-fed, fat cows. Then Pharaoh awoke.

Afterward he slept and had a second dream and saw seven ears, plump and good, growing up on one stalk. Also seven ears, thin and withered by the east wind, grew up after them. The thin ears swallowed up the seven plump, full ears. Then Pharaoh awoke, and knew that it was only a dream.

In the morning Pharaoh was worried. So he sent for all the magicians and wise men of Egypt and told them his dreams; but no one could tell him what they meant.

Then the chief butler said to Pharaoh, "I now remember my sins: Pharaoh was very angry with his servants and put me and the chief baker in prison in the house of the captain of the guard. We both had dreams the same night, each with a different meaning. There was also with us a young Hebrew, a servant of the captain of the guard. We told him our dreams and he told each of us what our dreams meant. And our dreams came true just as he said they would: I was restored to my office, but the chief baker was hanged."

Then Pharaoh sent for Joseph, and they quickly brought him out of the dungeon; and he shaved his face, changed his clothes, and came to Pharaoh. Pharaoh said to

Joseph, "I have had a dream, and there is no one who can tell what it means. Now I have heard that when you hear a dream, you can tell what it means." Joseph answered Pharaoh, "Not I; God alone can give Pharaoh a true answer."

Then Pharaoh said to Joseph, "In my dream as I stood on the bank of the Nile, I saw seven cows, fat and well fed, which had been feeding in the river grass. There came up after them seven more cows, poorly fed and thin, worse than I ever saw in all the land of Egypt; and the lean and poorly fed cows ate up the first seven fat cows. When they had eaten them up, one could not tell that they had eaten them, for they were still as thin as at the beginning. Then I awoke.

"Again I dreamed and saw seven ears, plump and good, grow up on one stalk; then seven thin ears, withered with the east wind, sprang up after them; and the thin ears swallowed up the seven good ears. I have told the dream to the magicians, but there is no one who can tell me what it means."

Then Joseph said to Pharaoh, "Pharaoh's two dreams mean the same thing; God has made known to Pharaoh what he is about to do. The seven good cows are seven years, and the seven good ears are seven years. It is one dream. The seven lean and poorly fed cows that came up after them are seven years, and the seven empty ears withered with the east wind mean seven years of famine. That is why I said to Pharaoh, 'God has shown to Pharaoh what he is about to do.' Seven years of great plenty all through the land of Egypt are coming. They shall be followed by seven years of famine, so that all the plenty will be forgotten in the land of Egypt. The famine will use up all that the land produces; and plenty will not be known in the land because of that famine which follows, for it will be very severe.

"The dream came twice to Pharaoh to show that the famine will surely come, and that God will soon make the dream come true. Now therefore let Pharaoh pick out a man who is sensible and wise and place him in charge of the land of Egypt. Let Pharaoh act quickly and put overseers over the land and collect one-fifth of all that grows in the land of Egypt in the seven years of plenty. Let them gather all the food of these good years that are coming and store up grain under the authority of Pharaoh, and let them hold it in the cities for food. The food will supply the land during the seven years of famine which shall be in the land of Egypt, so that the people of the land may not die because of the famine."

The plan pleased Pharaoh and all his people; and he said to his people, "Can we find one like this, a man in whom is the spirit of God?" So Pharaoh said to Joseph, "As God has shown you all this, there is no one so sensible and wise as you. You shall be at the head of my country, and all my people shall be ruled as you command. Only on the throne I will be above you."

So Pharaoh said to Joseph, "See, I have placed you over all the land of Egypt." And Pharaoh took off his signet-ring from his finger and put it upon Joseph's finger and clothed him in garments of fine linen and put a golden collar about his neck. He also made him ride in the second chariot which he had; and they cried before him, "Attention!" So he placed him over all the land of Egypt. Pharaoh also said to Joseph, "I am Pharaoh, but without your consent no man shall lift up his hand or his foot in all the land of Egypt." Pharaoh gave him as a wife Asenath, the daughter of Potiphera. And Joseph was thirty years old when he was made the ruler of the land of Egypt.

In the seven years of plenty there were large harvests, and Joseph gathered up all the food of the seven years of plenty, which were in the land of Egypt, and stored the food in the cities, putting in each city the food that grew in the fields about it. Joseph stored up grain as the sand of the sea, in great quantities, until he no longer kept account, because it could not be measured.

When the seven years of plenty in the land of Egypt were over, the seven years of famine began, as Joseph had said. There was famine in all lands, but all through the land of Egypt there was food, for when all the land of Egypt was hungry, the people cried to Pharaoh for bread, and Pharaoh said to all the Egyptians, "Go to Joseph and do what he tells you." So when the famine was over all the country, Joseph opened all the storehouses and sold food to the Egyptians: but the famine was severe in the land of Egypt. The peoples of all lands came to Joseph in Egypt to buy grain, for everywhere the famine was severe.

THE TESTING OF JOSEPH'S BROTHERS

When Jacob learned that there was grain for sale in Egypt, he said to his sons, "Why do you stand looking at each other? I have heard that there is grain for sale in Egypt; go down there and buy some for us, that we may live and not die." So Joseph's ten brothers went down to buy grain from Egypt. But Jacob did not send Benjamin, Joseph's own brother, with his brothers, for he feared that some harm might come to him. So the sons of Jacob went with others to buy grain, for the famine was in the land of Canaan.

Now Joseph was the governor over Egypt; it was he who sold grain to all the people of the land. So Joseph's brothers came and bowed before him with their faces to the earth. When Joseph saw his brothers, he knew them; but he acted as a stranger toward them and spoke harshly to them and said, "Where do you come from?" They said, "From the land of Canaan to buy food." So Joseph knew his brothers, but they did not know him.

Joseph also remembered the dreams which he had had about them and said to them, "You spies! you have come to see how defenseless the land is." But they said to him, "No, my lord; your servants have come to buy food. We are all sons of one man; we are honest men; your servants are not spies." But he again said to them, "No, you have come to see how defenseless the land is." They answered, "We, your servants, are twelve brothers, the sons of one father in the land of Canaan. The youngest is to-day with our father, and one is dead." Joseph said to them, "It is just as I said to you, 'You are spies.' By this you shall be tested: as sure as Pharaoh lives you shall not go away unless your youngest brother comes here. Send one of you, and let him bring your brother, while you remain in prison, that it may be proved whether you are telling the truth or not. Or else, as sure as Pharaoh lives, you are indeed spies."

So he put them all into prison for three days.

Then Joseph said to them on the third day, "Do this and live, for I fear God: if you are honest men, let one of your brothers stay in prison, but you go, carry grain for the needs of your households and bring your youngest brother to me. So you will prove that you have told the truth and you shall not die."

They did as Joseph commanded, but they said to one another, "We are indeed guilty because of the way we treated our brother, for when we saw his trouble and when he pleaded with us, we would not listen. That is why this trouble has come upon us." Reuben added, "Did I not say to you, 'Do not sin against the boy,' but you would not listen?"

They did not know, however, that Joseph understood them, for he had spoken to them through an interpreter. But he turned away from them and wept. Then he came back and spoke to them, and taking Simeon from among them, bound him before their eyes. Then Joseph gave orders to fill their vessels with grain and to put every man's money back in his sack and to give them food for the journey; and thus it was done to them. So they loaded their asses with their grain and went away.

When they came to Jacob their father in the land of Canaan, they told him all that had happened, saying, "The man who is master in that land spoke harshly to us and put us in prison as spies. We said to him, 'We are honest men; we are not spies; we are twelve brothers, sons of the same father; one is no longer living, and the youngest is to-day with our father in the land of Canaan.' But the man who is master in that land said to us, 'This is how I shall know that you are honest men: leave one of your brothers with me and take the grain to supply the needs of your households and go. Bring your youngest brother to me; then I shall know that you are not spies, but that you are honest men; and I will give your brother back to you and you shall be free to go about in the land.'"

As they were emptying their sacks, they found that each man's purse with his money was in his sack; and when they and their father saw their purses and the money, they were afraid and they turned trembling to one another with the question, "What is this that God has done to us?" Jacob their father said to them, "You have robbed me of my children: Joseph is no longer living and Simeon is no longer here, and now you would take Benjamin also! All this trouble has come to me!" But Reuben said to his father, "You may put my two sons to death, if I do not bring him to you. Put him in my charge and I will bring him back to you." Then Jacob said, "My son shall not go down with you, for his brother is dead and he only is left. If harm should come to him on the way by which you go, then you will bring down my gray hairs with sorrow to the grave."

The famine was severe in the land; and when Joseph's brothers had eaten up the grain which they had brought from Egypt, their father said to them, "Go again, buy us a little food." But Judah said to him, "The man plainly said to us: 'You shall not see me again unless your brother is with you.' If you will send our brother with us, we will go down and buy you food, but if you will not send him, we will not go down; for the man said to us, 'You shall not see me unless your brother is with you.'"

Jacob said, "Why did you bring trouble upon me by telling the man you had another brother?" They replied, "The man asked all about us and our family, saying, 'Is your father still alive? Have you another brother?' So we answered his questions as he asked them. How were we to know that he would say, 'Bring your brother down'?"

Then Judah said to Jacob, his father, "Send the lad with me, and we will go at once, that both we and you and our little ones may live and not die. I will be responsible for him; from me you may demand him. If I do not bring him to you and set him before you, let me bear the blame forever; for if we had not waited so long, surely we would by this time have come back the second time." So their father said to them, "If it must be so, then do this: take some of the fruits of the land in your jars and carry a present to the man, a little balsam, a little syrup, spices, ladanum, pistachio nuts, and almonds. Take twice as much money with you, carrying back the money that was put in your sacks. Perhaps it was a mistake. Take also your brother and go again to the man. May God Almighty grant that the man may be merciful to you and free Benjamin and your other brother. But if I am robbed of my sons, I am bereaved indeed!" So the men took the present and twice as much money and Benjamin, and went down to Egypt and stood before Joseph.

When Joseph saw Benjamin with them, he said to the steward of his house, "Bring the men into the house, kill animals, and prepare the meal, for these men will dine with me at noon." The steward did as Joseph ordered, and brought the men into Joseph's house. But the men were afraid, because they were brought into Joseph's house, and they said, "We are being brought in on account of the money that was put in our grain sacks at our first visit, that he may accuse us and fall upon us and take us as slaves, together with our asses."

So when they came near to Joseph's steward, they spoke to him at the door of the house and said, "Oh, my lord, we came down the first time only to buy food; but when we reached home, we opened our sacks and found that each man's money was in the mouth of his sack, our money in its full weight; and we have brought it back with us. We have brought down with us more money with which to buy food. We do not know who put our money into our sacks." He replied, "Peace be to you, fear not; your God and the God of your father has given you the treasure in your sacks; your money came to me."

Then he brought Simeon out to them. The steward also took the men to Joseph's house and gave them water with which to wash their feet, and he gave their asses fodder. Then they made ready the present for Joseph, when he should come at noon, for they had heard that they were to eat there.

When Joseph came into the house, they gave him the present which they had brought and bowed down low before him. He asked them about their welfare and said, "Is your father well, the old man of whom you spoke? Is he still living?" They replied, "Your servant, our father, is well; he is still alive." Then they bowed their heads and knelt down before him.

When Joseph looked up and saw Benjamin his brother, his own mother's son, he said, "Is this your youngest brother of whom you spoke to me?" And he added,

"God be gracious to you, my son." Then because of his longing for his brother he sought a place in which to weep. So he went into his room and wept there. Then he bathed his face and came out and said, "Bring on the food." So they brought food for him by himself and for them by themselves and for the Egyptians who ate with him by themselves, because the Egyptians would not eat with the Hebrews, for to do so was hateful to them.

Joseph's brothers were seated before him, the eldest first, as was his right as the oldest, and the youngest last, and the men looked at each other in astonishment. Then Joseph had portions served to them from the food before him. But Benjamin's portions were five times as much as any of theirs. So they drank and were merry with him.

Then he gave this command to the steward of his household: "Fill the men's grain sacks with food, as much as they can carry, and put my cup, the silver cup, in the mouth of the sack of the youngest and the money too that he paid for his grain." And the steward did as Joseph commanded.

As soon as the morning light appeared, the men were sent away with their asses. When they had gone out of the city, but were not yet far away, Joseph commanded his steward, "Follow after the men and when you overtake them, say to them, 'Why have you returned evil for good? Why have you stolen my silver cup, that from which my master drinks? You have done wrong in so doing.'"

So the steward overtook them and said these words to them. They said to him, "Why does my lord speak such words as these? Far be it from your servants to do such a thing! Remember that we brought back to you from the land of Canaan the money which we found in our sacks. Why then should we steal silver or gold from your master's house? Let that one of your servants with whom it is found die, and we will be my lord's slaves." He said, "Let it now be as you have said: he with whom it is found shall be my slave; but you shall be innocent." Then each one quickly took down his sack and opened it. The steward searched, beginning with the oldest and ending with the youngest; and the cup was found in Benjamin's sack. Then they tore their clothes, and every man loaded his ass and returned to the city.

JOSEPH'S FORGIVENESS OF HIS BROTHERS

When Judah and his brothers came back to Joseph's house, Joseph was still there; and they threw themselves before him on the ground. Joseph said to them, "What deed is this that you have done? Do you not know that a man like me can always tell where things are?" Judah replied, "What shall we say to my lord? What shall we speak or how shall we clear ourselves? God has found out the guilt of your servants. See, both we and he also with whom the cup was found are my lord's slaves." But Joseph said, "Far be it from me that I should do so! The man with whom the cup was found shall be my slave; but you yourselves go up in peace to your father."

Then Judah came close to him and said, "Oh, my lord, let your servant, I beg of you, speak a word in my lord's ears, and let not your anger be aroused against your servant, for you are even as Pharaoh. My lord asked his servants, saying, 'Have you a father or a brother?' And we said to my lord, 'We have a father, an old man, and a child of his old age, a little one. As his brother is dead, he is the only son of his mother who is left; and his father loves him.' You said to your servants, 'Bring him down to me, that I may see him.' But we said to my lord, 'The boy cannot leave his father; for if he should leave his father, his father would die.' Then you said to your servants, 'Unless your youngest brother comes down with you, you shall not see me again.'

"When we went up to your servant, my father, we told him the words of my lord; and our father said, 'Go again, buy us a little food.' But we said, 'We cannot go down. If our youngest brother is with us, then we will go; for we cannot see the man again unless our youngest brother is with us.' Your servant, my father, said to us, 'You know that my wife had two sons; and one went from me,' and I said, 'Surely he is torn in pieces; and I have not seen him since. If you take this one also from me, and harm come to him, you will bring down my gray hairs with sorrow to the grave.' Now if I return to your servant, my father, and Benjamin with whose life his heart is bound up is not with us, and he sees that there is no boy, he will die, and your servants will bring down the gray hairs of your servant our father with sorrow to the grave. For your servant became responsible for the boy to my father, when I said, 'If I do not bring him to you, then I will bear the blame before my father forever.' Now, therefore, let me, instead of the boy, remain as a slave to my lord, I beg of you; but let the boy go back with his brothers. For how can I go back to my father, if the boy is not with me, lest I should see the sorrow that would come upon my father?"

Then Joseph could not control himself before all those who were standing by him; so he cried out, "Let every man leave me." So no Egyptian was present while Joseph made himself known to his brothers. But he wept so loudly that the Egyptians and Pharaoh's court heard.

And Joseph said to his brothers, "I am Joseph. Is my father still alive?" But his brothers could not answer him, for they were too ashamed to look him in the face. Then Joseph said to his brothers, "Come near to me, I beg of you." So they came near. He said, "I am Joseph, your brother, whom you sold into Egypt. Do not be troubled nor angry with yourselves that you sold me here, for God sent me before you to save your lives. For the famine has already been two years in the land, and there are still five years in which there shall be neither ploughing nor harvest. God sent me before you to save your lives through a great deliverance and thus give you children on the earth. So now it is not you who sent me here, but God. He has made me like a father to Pharaoh and master of all his household and ruler over all the land of Egypt.

"Go up quickly to my father and say to him, 'Your son Joseph says: God has made me master of all Egypt. Come down to me without delay. You shall live in the land of Goshen, and you shall be near me with your children and your grandchildren, with your flocks and your herds and all that you have, so that you, with your household and all that you have, may never want. There I will provide for you, for there will be five more years of famine.' Now you and my brother Benjamin see that it is I who am speaking to you. Tell my father all about my honor in Egypt and what you have seen; and you must quickly bring him down here."

Then he fell upon his brother Benjamin's neck and wept, and Benjamin wept upon his neck. He also kissed all his brothers and wept upon them. After that his brothers talked with him.

JOSEPH'S LOYALTY TO HIS FAMILY

The news that Joseph's brothers had arrived became known in Pharaoh's palace; and it pleased Pharaoh and his servants greatly. Pharaoh said to Joseph, "Say to your brothers, 'Do this: load your beasts, go to the land of Canaan, and take your father and your families and come to me, and I will give you the best there is in the land of Egypt, and you shall eat the best that the land can give. Now you are commanded to do this: take wagons from the land of Egypt for your little ones and for your wives, and bring your father and come. Also do not pay any attention to your household goods, for the best of all there is in the land of Egypt is yours.'" And the sons of Jacob did as they were commanded.

So Joseph gave them wagons, as Pharaoh ordered, and what was needed for the journey. To each of them he gave a change of clothing, but to Benjamin he gave three hundred pieces of silver and five changes of clothing. To his father he sent this gift: ten asses loaded with the best products of Egypt and ten asses loaded with grain and bread and provisions for his father on the journey.

So he sent his brothers away, and, as they went, he said to them, "See that you do not quarrel on the journey!" So they went up out of Egypt and came into the land of Canaan to Jacob their father, and told him, "Joseph is still alive, and he is ruler over all the land of Egypt!" Then Jacob's heart stood still, for he could not believe them. But when they told him all that Joseph had said to them and when he saw the wagons which Joseph had sent to carry him, the spirit of Jacob their father revived, and he said, "It is enough; Joseph my son is still alive. I will go and see him before I die."

Then Jacob set out on his journey with all that he had. He first went to Beersheba and offered sacrifices to the God of his father Isaac. God spoke to him in a vision by night and said, "Jacob, Jacob." He answered, "Here am I." God said, "I am God, the God of your father. Do not fear to go down into Egypt, for there I will make of you a great nation. I myself will go down with you into Egypt; I will surely bring you back again; and Joseph shall close your dying eyes."

When Jacob left Beersheba, his sons carried him and their little ones and their wives in the wagons that Pharaoh had sent. Jacob also sent Judah before him to Joseph, that he might show him the way to Goshen.

When they came into the land of Goshen, Joseph made ready his chariot, and went up to Goshen to meet Jacob his father. When he met him, Jacob fell on his neck and wept there a long time.

Then Jacob said to Joseph, "Now let me die, for I have seen your face and know that you are still alive." But Joseph said to his brothers and to his father's household, "I will go up and tell Pharaoh and will say to him, 'My brothers and my father's family who were in the land of Canaan have come to me. Now the men are shepherds, for they have been keepers of cattle; and they have brought their flocks and cattle and all that they have.' When Pharaoh calls you, and asks, 'What is your business?' you shall say, 'Your servants have been keepers of cattle from our youth even until now, both we and our fathers.' Say this that you may live in the land of Goshen, for every shepherd is looked down upon by the Egyptians."

Then Joseph went in and told Pharaoh and said, "My father and my brothers with their sheep and cattle and all that they possess have come from the land of Canaan; and now they are in the province of Goshen." And he took five of his brothers and presented them to Pharaoh. Pharaoh said to them, "What is your business?" They answered, "Your servants are shepherds, both we and our fathers." They also said to Pharaoh, "We have come to live in your country; because the famine is severe in the land of Canaan, and there is no pasture for your servants' flocks. Now, therefore, we beg of you, let your servants stay in the land of Goshen."

Then Pharaoh said to Joseph, "Let them stay in the land of Goshen; and if you know any able men among them, put them in charge of my cattle."

Joseph also brought in Jacob his father and presented him to Pharaoh; and Jacob blessed Pharaoh. Then Pharaoh said to Jacob, "How many years have you lived?" Jacob answered, "I have lived a hundred and thirty years; few and evil have been the years of my life, and they have not been as many as those that my forefathers lived on earth." After Jacob had blessed Pharaoh, he went out from Pharaoh's presence. So Joseph gave his father and his brothers a place to live in and a home in the land of Goshen, in the best part of the land of Egypt, as Pharaoh had commanded.

Joseph also provided food for his father and his brothers and all his father's family according to the number of the little children. So the Israelites lived in Egypt, in the land of Goshen, and there they grew wealthy and had many children.